Put Beginning Readers on the Right Track with
ALL ABOARD READING™

The All Aboard Reading series is especially for beginning readers. Written by noted authors and illustrated in full color, these are books that children really and truly *want* to read—books to excite their imagination, tickle their funny bone, expand their interests, and support their feelings. With four different reading levels, All Aboard Reading lets you choose which books are most appropriate for your children and their growing abilities.

Picture Readers—for Ages 3 to 6
Picture Readers have super-simple texts, with many nouns appearing as rebus pictures. At the end of each book are 24 flash cards—on one side is the rebus picture; on the other side is the written-out word.

Level 1—for Preschool through First-Grade Children
Level 1 books have very few lines per page, very large type, easy words, lots of repetition, and pictures with visual "cues" to help children figure out the words on the page.

Level 2—for First-Grade to Third-Grade Children
Level 2 books are printed in slightly smaller type than Level 1 books. The stories are more complex, but there is still lots of repetition in the text, and many pictures. The sentences are quite simple and are broken up into short lines to make reading easier.

Level 3—for Second-Grade through Third-Grade Children
Level 3 books have considerably longer texts, harder words, and more complicated sentences.

All Aboard for happy reading!

For my father and
in memory of my mother—F. E. R.

For Mary, John, Daisy, and Gary,
good friends all—S. M.

Photo credits: title page, Bob Adelman / Magnum Photos; p. 7, Bettmann / Corbis; p. 14-15, Leonard Freed / Magnum Photos; p. 16, Bettmann / Corbis; p. 18, Bettmann / Corbis; p. 19, Danny Lyon / Magnum Photos; p. 22-23, Charles Moore / Black Star; p. 24, UPI-Bettmann / Corbis; p. 26-27, Bettmann / Corbis; p. 32, Bruce Davidson / Magnum Photos; p. 36-37, UPI-Bettmann / Corbis; p. 40, Bruce Davidson / Magnum Photos; p. 48, Fred Ward / Black Star

Library of Congress Cataloging-in-Publication Data
Ruffin, Frances E.
    Martin Luther King, Jr. and the march on Washington / by Frances E. Ruffin ; illustrated by Stephen Marchesi.
        p.   cm. — (All aboard reading)
    1. King, Martin Luther, Jr., 1929–1968—Juvenile literature. 2. March on Washington for Jobs and Freedom, Washington, D.C., 1963—Juvenile literature. 3. Afro-Americans—Civil rights—History—20th century—Juvenile literature. 4. Civil rights movements—United States—History—20th century—Juvenile literature. [1. King, Martin Luther, Jr., 1929–1968—Juvenile literature. 2. March on Washington for Jobs and Freedom, Washington, D.C., 1963. 3. Afro-Americans—Civil rights. 4. Civil rights demonstrations.]
I. Marchesi, Stephen, ill. II. Title. III. Series
    E185.97.K5 R84 2001
    323'.092—dc21
    [B]   00-057304

ISBN 0-448-42424-X (GB)   A B C D E F G H I J
ISBN 0-448-42421-5 (pbk)   A B C D E F G H I J

ALL ABOARD READING™

Level 2
Grades 1-3

MARTIN LUTHER KING, Jr.

and the March on Washington

By Frances E. Ruffin
Illustrated by Stephen Marchesi

Grosset & Dunlap • New York

August 28, 1963

It is a hot summer day
in Washington, D.C.
More than 250,000 people
are pouring into the city.
They have come by plane,
by train,
by car,
and by bus.

Some people have walked all the way
to Washington from New York City.
That's more than 230 miles.

One man has roller-skated

from Chicago.

It has taken him eleven days!

By late morning,

a crowd has gathered at one end

of a long, narrow pool.

Nearby is the Lincoln Memorial

with its statue of Abraham Lincoln.

Why are so many people here

at this place on this day?

It is because one hundred years ago,

President Lincoln helped

to free the people who were slaves.

It was during the Civil War.

President Lincoln knew that

slavery had to end.

Now it is 1963.

There has been no slavery

for a long time.

But are black people

and white people treated equally?

No.

And that is why

people are in Washington today.

They have come to protest.

They will speak out against

something they think is wrong.

In the South and in some other states, there are laws to keep

black people and white people apart.

Black people cannot eat

in many restaurants

or stay in many hotels.

In movie theaters,

they must enter by separate doors

and sit way up in the balcony.

On public buses,

they have to take seats

in the back.

There are signs that say,

"For Whites Only."

Even water fountains say

"White" or "Colored."

Which of these fountains
looks nicer to you?

Black people and many white people
want things to change.
It is time for a change.
It is <u>past</u> time for a change.

In the crowd are some grandchildren
and great-grandchildren of slaves.
Many of these people have been
part of protests before.

AW SAYS!
END
EGREGATED
RULES
IN
PUBLIC
CHOOLS

I.U.E
FOR
FULL
EMPLOYMENT

There have been sit-ins in many cities.

At sit-ins, black people take seats

in "white only" restaurants or theaters.

And they refuse to leave.

Often they are dragged out.

Sometimes they are put in jail.

There have been protest marches

in many Southern cities and towns.

People hold signs.

They sing songs.

But what if everyone got together

in one place to protest?

That is the idea of

two black leaders named

A. Philip Randolph and Bayard Rustin.

They pick Washington, D.C.

as the place.

It is the nation's capital.

It is where laws are made.

So, on August 28, 1963,

at 11:30 a.m.,

the March on Washington begins.

The crowd marches

to the Lincoln Memorial.

As they walk, the people sing:

We shall overcome,

We shall overcome,

We shall overcome someday.

Later, there are many speakers.

They stand on the steps

of the memorial,

in front of Lincoln's statue.

Each person talks about freedom.

The marchers sit on the grass

and listen.

They know that today

history is being made.

By noon, the sun is very hot.

Some people take off their shoes

and cool their feet in the pool.

Bag lunches are sold.

Each one has a cheese sandwich,

an apple, and a slice of pound cake—

all for fifty cents.

The high point of the day

comes at three o'clock.

The crowd grows quiet.

A young black man takes the stage.

He looks at the crowd.

There are people as far as he can see.

The man's name is
Martin Luther King, Jr.
He is a preacher and
the son of a preacher.
He has grown up in Georgia.
He knows all about what it is like
to be a black person in the South.

Dr. King is a man of peace.

But he is also a fighter.

He doesn't use his fists

or weapons.

He uses words.

In the South,

Dr. King has led

many other protests.

One was a march

in Georgia.

Another was a protest

against a bus company

in Alabama.

He has been put in jail

many times.

There are threats against his life.

Some people want him dead.

But that does not stop him.

Today, in Washington,

Dr. King speaks words of hope.

His speech is about his dream

for a better world.

He says,

"I have a dream that

my four little children

will one day live in a nation

where they will not be judged

by the color of their skin. . . ."

He hopes that people will see

all children for who they are,

and for the things they do

in their lives.

It is his dream that one day

"little black boys and black girls

will be able to join hands

with little white boys and girls."

Dr. King speaks for

16 minutes and 20 seconds.

His voice rises and falls.

The crowd leans forward.

They want to hear every word.

Nine times Dr. King says,

"I have a dream."

When Dr. King finishes,

there is silence.

Then 250,000 people

start to clap and to cheer.

Some people are so moved

by his words, they cry.

People all around the world watch

Martin Luther King, Jr. on TV.

So does President John F. Kennedy.

By early evening,

people start back to their cars,

to the buses,

and to the trains and planes.

It is time to go home.

The march has ended.

But that is not the end of the story.

One year later,

a law is passed.

It is called

the Civil Rights Act of 1964.

From now on,

there cannot be restaurants

for "whites only."

There cannot be separate seating

for black people and white people

in any public place.

People cannot be kept apart

just because of their skin color.

It does not change everything.

But it is a beginning.

And the power of words,

the words of Dr. King and others,

changes the law of the land.